SHARKS, RAYS, and EELS

A GOLDEN JUNIOR GUIDE®

SHARKS, RAYS, and EELS

By CHRISTOPHER LAMPTON

Illustrated by BARBARA HOOPES AMBLER

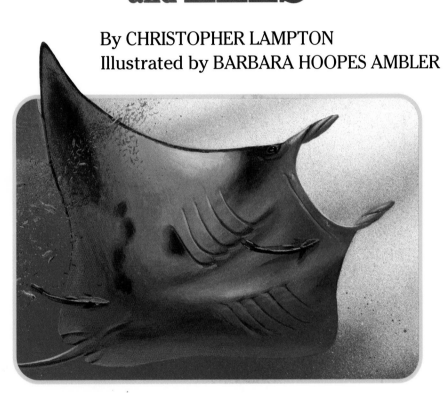

Consultant: Dr. George Benz, Curator of Fishes, Tennessee Aquarium

A GOLDEN BOOK • NEW YORK

Western Publishing Company, Inc., Racine, Wisconsin 53404

Sharks, Rays, and Eels are some of the strangest and most frightening creatures on earth. Like other fish, they spend just about all of their lives underwater, breathing through special openings in their heads called *gill slits*. Their fins, which stick out from their bodies a little like arms or legs, help them to swim. In this book you will meet some of the most common—and most unusual—sharks, rays, and eels.

Blue Shark

Sharks attack less than 100 people each year. Still, they are feared throughout the world. Blue Sharks, which are quite common, are about 13 feet long. They swim far out at sea, feeding mostly on squid and small fish.

Sharks, Rays, and Eels all have gill slits and fins in various places on their bodies. Each type of fin has a different name. Besides helping them to swim, fins help fish keep their balance and steer.

Gray Nurse Shark

dorsal fin

caudal fin

gill slits

pectoral fin

pelvic fin

anal fin

Squid

Did You Know?
People kill sharks for food, oil, sport, or in hopes of protecting the fish *they* want to catch. One result of all this killing is that some kinds of sharks are becoming scarce.

All Fish

All Fish have certain things in common, such as fins and gill slits. But there are many important differences between various groups of fish. Following are some of the features that can help you tell apart sharks, rays, and eels.

Sharks

- ❏ Shark skeletons are made of cartilage. (Most fish have bony skeletons.) This is the same flexible material your ears are made of.
- ❏ Sharks have five or more gill slits on each side of their head.
- ❏ Sharks have large, stiff fins on their back. These sometimes stick up above the water when the shark swims near the surface.
- ❏ Most sharks have a teardrop- or cigar-shaped body.

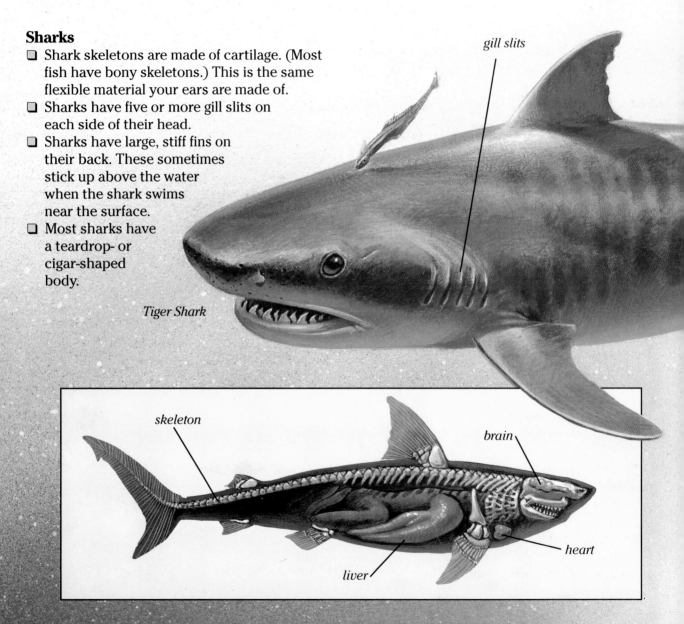

gill slits

Tiger Shark

skeleton

brain

heart

liver

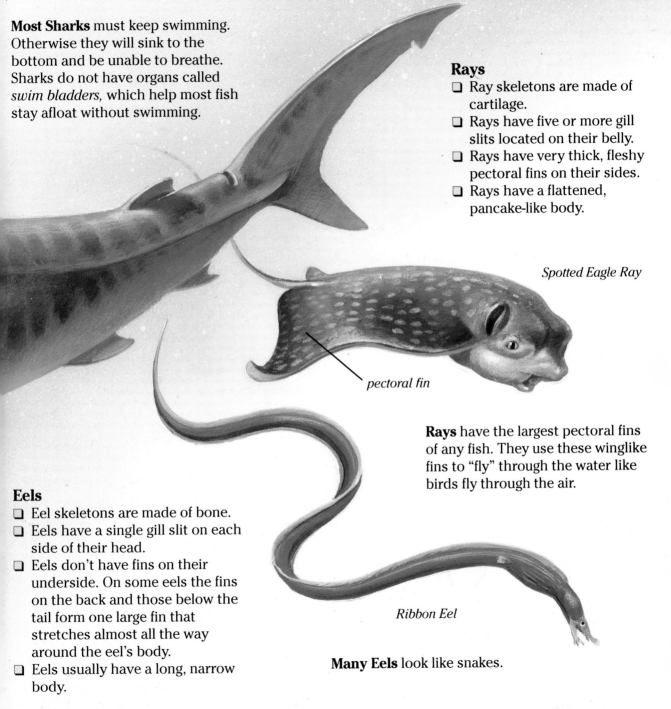

Most Sharks must keep swimming. Otherwise they will sink to the bottom and be unable to breathe. Sharks do not have organs called *swim bladders,* which help most fish stay afloat without swimming.

Rays

- ❏ Ray skeletons are made of cartilage.
- ❏ Rays have five or more gill slits located on their belly.
- ❏ Rays have very thick, fleshy pectoral fins on their sides.
- ❏ Rays have a flattened, pancake-like body.

Spotted Eagle Ray

pectoral fin

Rays have the largest pectoral fins of any fish. They use these winglike fins to "fly" through the water like birds fly through the air.

Eels

- ❏ Eel skeletons are made of bone.
- ❏ Eels have a single gill slit on each side of their head.
- ❏ Eels don't have fins on their underside. On some eels the fins on the back and those below the tail form one large fin that stretches almost all the way around the eel's body.
- ❏ Eels usually have a long, narrow body.

Ribbon Eel

Many Eels look like snakes.

Sharks

Sharks are very ancient fish. They had already been around for 200 million years when the first dinosaurs appeared on earth. Because a shark's skeleton is made of cartilage rather than bone, it is light and flexible. Most sharks can swim fast—some more than 40 miles an hour. There are about 350 different kinds of sharks. Almost all eat other animals, and some are fierce hunters.

baby Lemon Shark

Did You Know?

Some sharks, when they are hungry, will eat whatever is floating in the water—an old boot, clothing, even cardboard. Sharks don't chew their food. They bite off a chunk and swallow it whole.

Most Sharks give birth to live babies, called *pups,* which immediately swim away from their mother. Some sharks lay *egg cases.* When the baby shark is fully developed, it bursts out of the case and swims off.

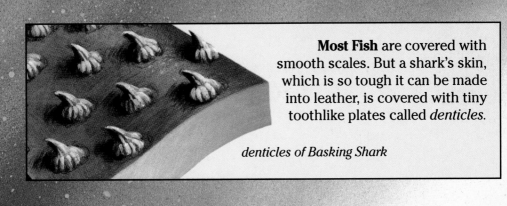

Most Fish are covered with smooth scales. But a shark's skin, which is so tough it can be made into leather, is covered with tiny toothlike plates called *denticles*.

denticles of Basking Shark

puffer fish

Sharks have few natural enemies. People and other sharks pose the greatest threats. But sharks will usually avoid eating the spiny puffer fish, which can blow itself up inside the shark's throat and choke it.

adult Lemon Shark

Great White Sharks, which are also known as the White Death, are usually found in cool ocean waters. A few may reach lengths of 30 feet and weigh nearly 10,000 pounds. The teeth of the Great White can be up to 3 inches long—the length of a pocket knife—and very sharp. Great Whites live for about 20 years. They eat seals, large fish, and injured whales. The larger Great Whites can swallow a seal whole. Great Whites do attack people, but not very often.

Great White Shark

A Great White Shark is an eating machine. It will gobble up just about anything that swims, including fish, turtles, sea lions, and even other sharks.

Did You Know?
A Great White can smell a single drop of blood in 25 gallons of water. One injured fish can attract sharks for many miles around. Hungry sharks approaching prey sometimes get so excited by the smell of blood that they will bite each other!

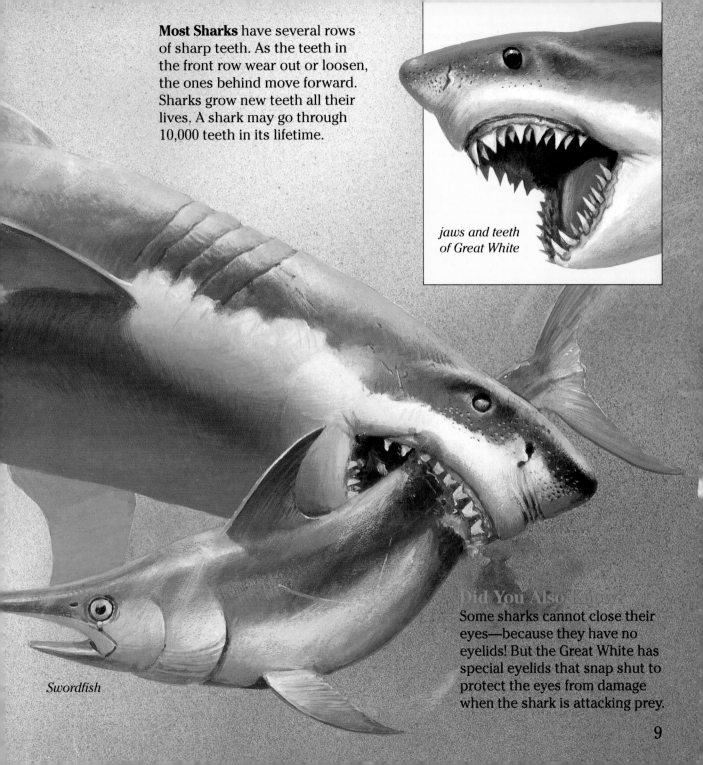

Most Sharks have several rows of sharp teeth. As the teeth in the front row wear out or loosen, the ones behind move forward. Sharks grow new teeth all their lives. A shark may go through 10,000 teeth in its lifetime.

jaws and teeth of Great White

Swordfish

Some sharks cannot close their eyes—because they have no eyelids! But the Great White has special eyelids that snap shut to protect the eyes from damage when the shark is attacking prey.

Bull Sharks are dangerous! They can grow to 10 feet long and weigh 500 pounds. Although they are not as large or as famous as the Great White, they like to swim in the shallow waters near land. Therefore, they probably attack people more often. Females can have up to a dozen pups at a time. Bull Sharks are unusual because they sometimes leave the salty water of the ocean to live in fresh water. In the United States, Bull Sharks have been spotted in the Mississippi River.

Bull Shark

Did You Know?
Sharks often swim with smaller fish, such as Pilotfish, which eat any bits of flesh left over from whatever the shark has attacked.

Bull Sharks like to swim in rivers. Because of this, they sometimes attack animals other sharks never even get near, such as cattle and rhinoceroses!

Bull Sharks may sometimes be preyed upon by Killer Whales. A Killer Whale is one of the few animals large enough and aggressive enough to frighten a Bull Shark.

Whale Sharks

are the largest fish in the world. They can reach lengths of at least 40 feet. This is longer than a moving van! Whale Sharks feed on small fish and other tiny animals they capture as they swim along with their mouth open. These prey are strained from the water by comblike structures called *gill rakers* inside the shark's mouth. Whale Sharks are found in warm ocean waters around the world. They like to swim in large groups far out at sea. Some Whale Sharks like to swim near the surface of the water and will sometimes bump into boats.

Whale Sharks

Whale Sharks are peaceful and don't attack people. Some will even let divers ride on their backs.

Sharks never stop growing. They just keep getting bigger all their lives. But as they get older, they grow slower and slower—until they hardly grow at all.

Dwarf Dogsharks are the smallest known sharks, reaching lengths of only about 8 inches. Pygmy Sharks and Cigar Sharks are also less than 12 inches long.

Dwarf Dogshark

Shortfin Mako Sharks

Shortfin Mako Sharks are the speed demons of the shark world. They can swim very fast and leap 20 feet into the air. Makos are found in warm ocean waters, where the adult feeds mainly on large fish such as tuna and swordfish. Baby makos feed on small fish and squid. While still inside the mother, the unborn pups will sometimes gobble up the eggs that the mother continues to produce. Makos are a popular food shark.

Shortfin Mako Shark

The Shortfin Mako grows to lengths of about 13 feet. Though some regard it as a dangerous shark, it is rarely found close to shore, where most people swim.

Many Sharks have teeth shaped like triangles, but the curved teeth of the Shortfin Mako are long and thin. Prey grabbed by these teeth are not likely to get away!

Mako teeth

15

Hammerhead Sharks

Hammerhead Sharks are very strange-looking. Their eyes are at the ends of stalks that stick out on both sides of their head. Like most other sharks, hammerheads can detect the slight electrical currents given off by fish and other animals. The oddly shaped head may serve as a kind of detector for locating prey, picking up electrical signals like a TV antenna does. There are nine different kinds of hammerheads. One is almost 20 feet long, but most are less than 6 feet.

Great Hammerhead Shark

Hammerheads often go after fish, including stingrays, hiding in the sandy bottom of the ocean. The poisonous barb, or spine, that the stingray uses to defend itself does not seem to bother the hammerhead at all.

16

Did You Know?

Sharks will sometimes take bites out of boats. The metal in the boat produces an electrical field. This may confuse the shark into thinking the boat is really a large fish.

school of Bonnetheads

These Hammerheads, called Bonnetheads, travel in large schools, patrolling the shallow waters near the shore.

spine

Atlantic Stingray

17

Thresher Sharks

Thresher Sharks can grow to 20 feet long, but half this length is in their long, whiplike tail. Threshers are found in both cool and warm waters around the world. They like to swim in deep water but will chase schools of fish almost all the way to land. Threshers are very long-lived sharks. Some may survive for up to 50 years.

Thresher Sharks

Thresher Sharks use their tail fin like a whip to stun schools of small fish. The last flick may send the fish right into the Thresher's mouth!

18

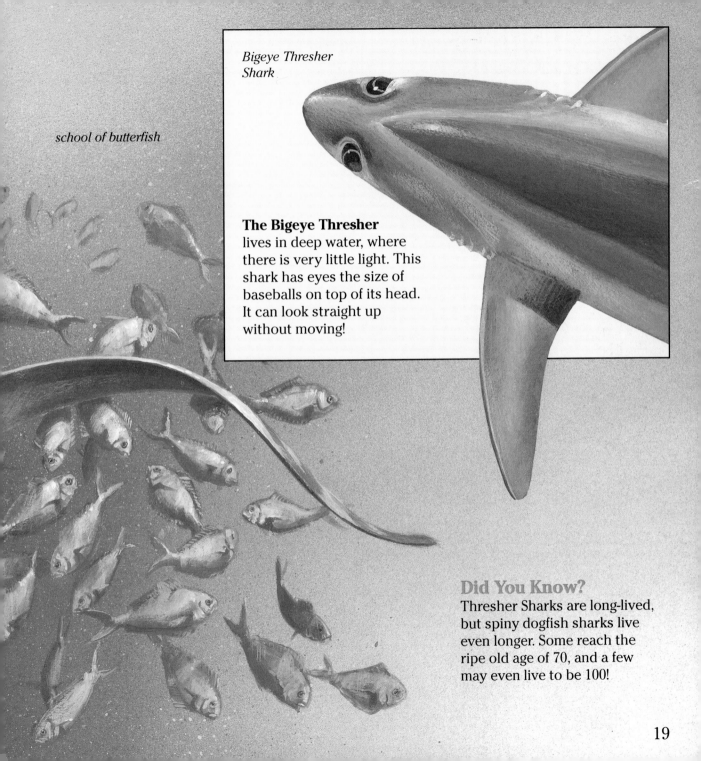

school of butterfish

*Bigeye Thresher
Shark*

The Bigeye Thresher
lives in deep water, where
there is very little light. This
shark has eyes the size of
baseballs on top of its head.
It can look straight up
without moving!

Did You Know?
Thresher Sharks are long-lived,
but spiny dogfish sharks live
even longer. Some reach the
ripe old age of 70, and a few
may even live to be 100!

19

Cookiecutter Sharks

Cookiecutter Sharks are only about 2 feet long, but they often take bites out of fish much bigger than themselves. They will sometimes even bite into the rubber parts of a submarine, perhaps thinking it is a whale! The small shark's jaws nearly pop out of its mouth to form a suction cup that attaches to the skin of the other fish. Then the Cookiecutter cuts small, neat round holes out of the fish's flesh—the way a cookie cutter cuts cookie dough!

Cookiecutters love to eat whale blubber. They will even go after the giant Whale Shark!

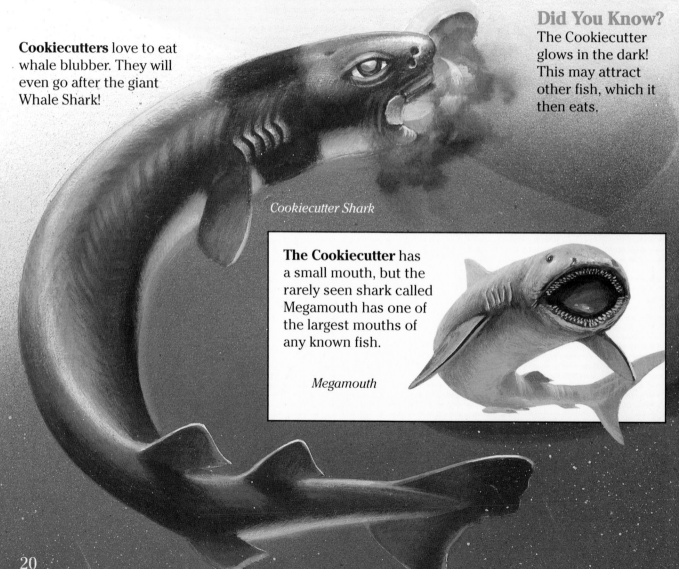

Cookiecutter Shark

Did You Know?
The Cookiecutter glows in the dark! This may attract other fish, which it then eats.

The Cookiecutter has a small mouth, but the rarely seen shark called Megamouth has one of the largest mouths of any known fish.

Megamouth

Wobbegong Sharks

Wobbegong Sharks belong to a group of fish known as *carpet sharks*. These creatures spend nearly all of their lives on the ocean bottom, lying flat like rugs. Because they blend in so completely with their surroundings, they are able to capture unsuspecting small fish and shellfish swimming nearby. Wobbegongs like shallow water and, looking for slow-moving prey, will sometimes crawl between tide pools.

school of Nurse Sharks

Carpet Sharks called Nurse Sharks often gather together in shallow waters to form a living "shark carpet."

Wobbegong Sharks, found mainly in Australia, grow up to 10 feet long. The Wobbegong has a "beard" that looks like sea growth. When tiny fish come up to nibble on it, the Wobbegong eats them!

Tasselled Wobbegong Shark

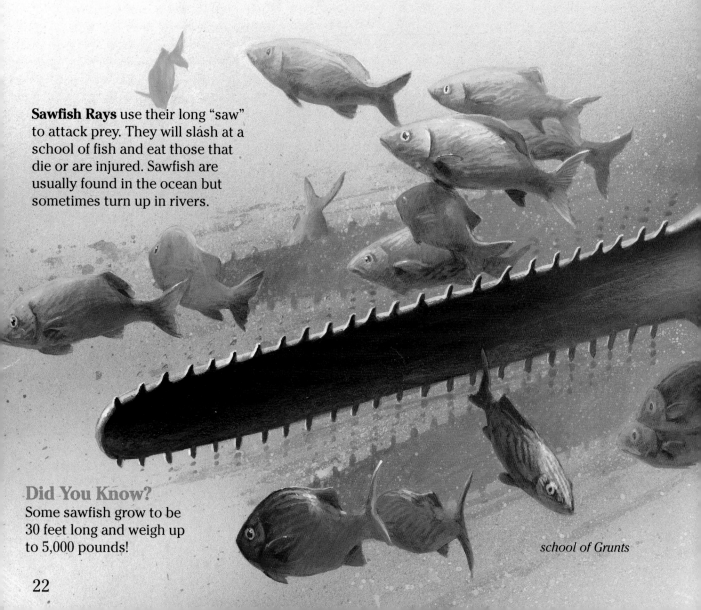

Rays are close relatives of sharks. Like sharks, they have skeletons made of cartilage. But they also have flattened bodies and fins that flap like wings when they swim. Rays can often be found on the seabed, eating shellfish and worms. Some have patterns on their back that make them hard to see as they rest or search for food on the seafloor. Some rays, however, are fierce predators.

Sawfish Rays use their long "saw" to attack prey. They will slash at a school of fish and eat those that die or are injured. Sawfish are usually found in the ocean but sometimes turn up in rivers.

Did You Know?
Some sawfish grow to be 30 feet long and weigh up to 5,000 pounds!

school of Grunts

22

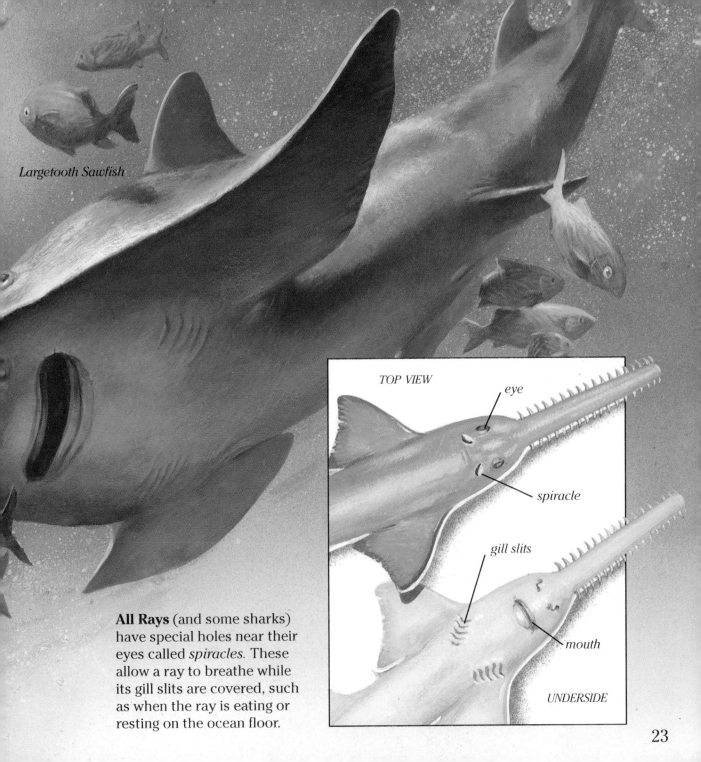

Largetooth Sawfish

All Rays (and some sharks) have special holes near their eyes called _spiracles_. These allow a ray to breathe while its gill slits are covered, such as when the ray is eating or resting on the ocean floor.

TOP VIEW

eye

spiracle

gill slits

mouth

UNDERSIDE

23

Manta Rays

are the largest rays. With fins outstretched, a big Manta can measure more than 20 feet across. This is larger than the wingspan of a small airplane! Because the fins on their head can curl up to look like horns, Mantas have a rather devilish look and are sometimes even called "devilfish." But they are actually quite gentle. They swim fast and can leap high above the waves. Mantas can be found in all warm ocean waters.

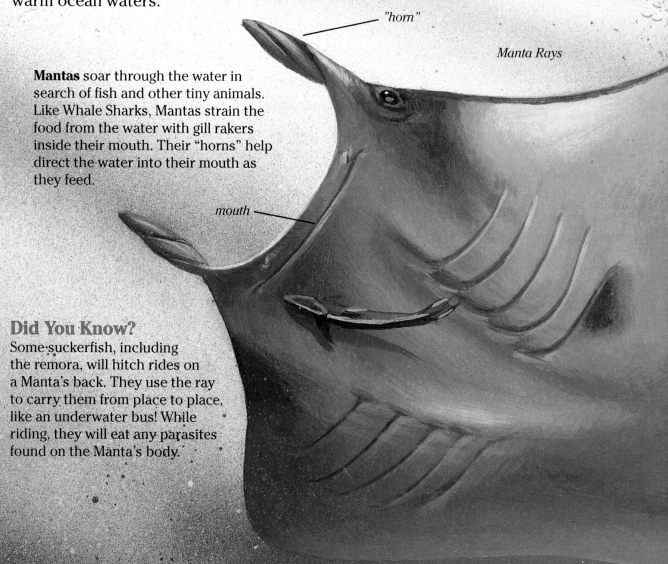

"horn"

Manta Rays

Mantas soar through the water in search of fish and other tiny animals. Like Whale Sharks, Mantas strain the food from the water with gill rakers inside their mouth. Their "horns" help direct the water into their mouth as they feed.

mouth

Did You Know?

Some suckerfish, including the remora, will hitch rides on a Manta's back. They use the ray to carry them from place to place, like an underwater bus! While riding, they will eat any parasites found on the Manta's body.

Did You Also Know?
Mantas are the only rays known to leap high out of the water. Sometimes during these leaps, a Manta mother will give birth to her young.

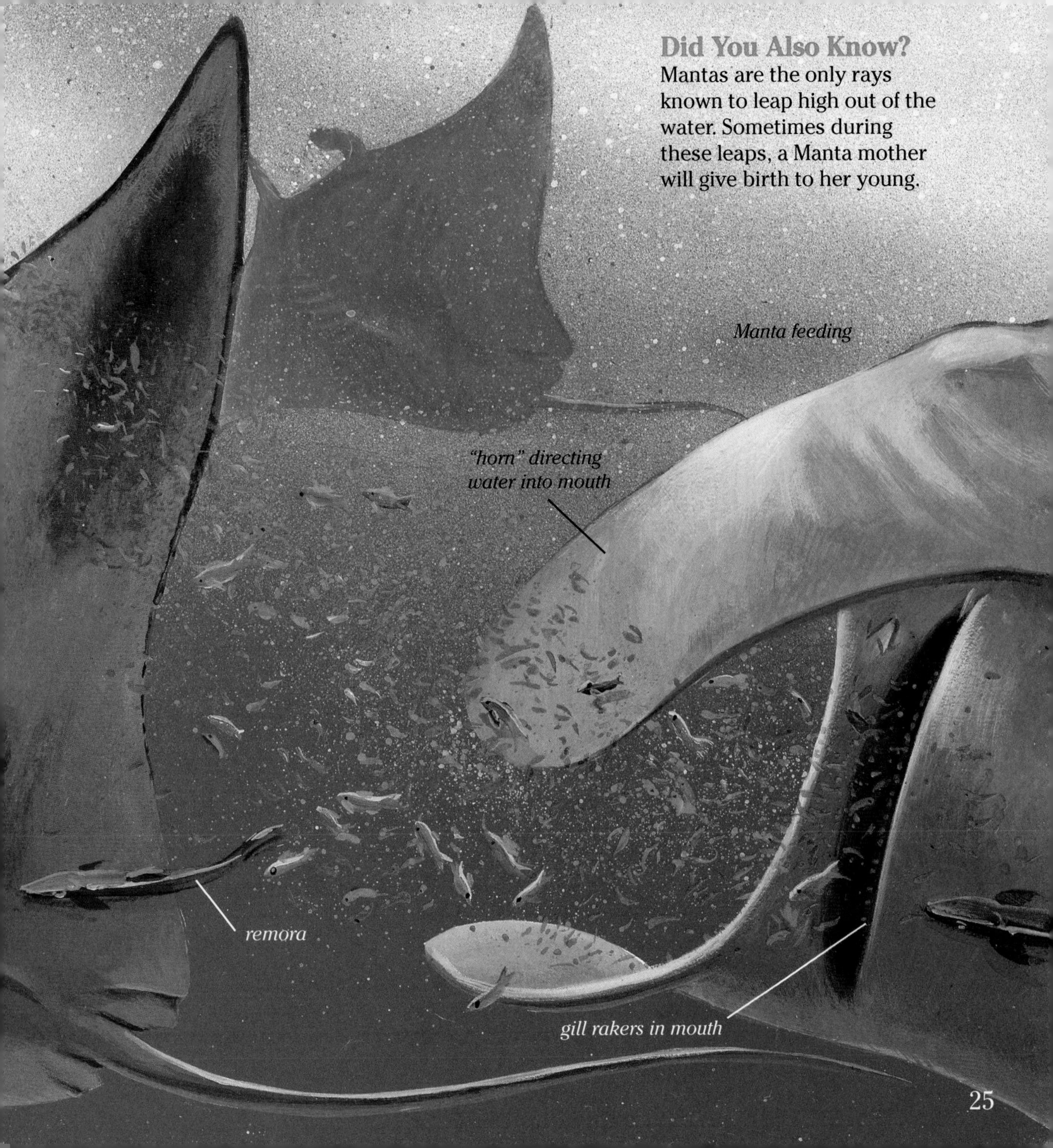

Manta feeding

"horn" directing water into mouth

remora

gill rakers in mouth

25

Stingrays

Stingrays get their name from the poisonous spines on their tail. These "stingers" are used by the stingray to defend itself. Stingrays eat mostly mollusks such as snails and clams. Their teeth are hard and flat—perfect for cracking the shells open. Like Mantas, stingrays are found in warm ocean waters around the world.

Dusky Shark

tail

spine

A Stingray, under attack, will stick its spines in the attacker's flesh. Once in, these spines are hard to get out. And the poison makes the wound very painful, even deadly.

Some Stingrays measure 15 feet long and weigh more than 750 pounds. The spines of such large stingrays, washed up on shore, can kill beachgoers who step on them by accident.

Indo-Pacific Smooth Stingray

Southern Stingray

Electric Rays

Electric Rays are like underwater power plants. Some kinds can produce a brief jolt of more than 200 volts of electricity. This is enough to stun or kill prey or scare off a predator. (The electrical outlets in your home supply 120 volts each.) There are many different types of electric rays. Some are only 1 foot long; others grow to 6 feet. Electric rays are found in shallow waters around the world.

Electric Rays produce electricity using special organs on their head.

organ that produces electricity

Atlantic Torpedo Ray stunning its prey

Did You Know?
Electric rays are not the only fish that can produce strong jolts of electricity. Electric Eels, Electric Catfish, and some kinds of stargazer fish can do it, too.

Guitarfish

Guitarfish get their name from the guitarlike shape of their body. Guitarfish are close relatives of electric rays and stingrays but look more like sawfish rays without the saws. Like stingrays, guitarfish have hard, flat teeth for cracking the shells of clams, snails, lobsters, and other shellfish.

Atlantic Guitarfish

Some Guitarfish are the color of sand. This helps them blend in with the ocean bottom. Like most rays, guitarfish live mainly in shallow coastal waters.

Did You Know?
Skates, a closely related group of fish, have large thorny scales on their back and along their tail. These are used to protect the skates from being eaten by other fish.

Eels

Eels do not look like either sharks or rays. But they can be just as dangerous and frightening. Some well-known "eels," by the way, are not true eels. Electric Eels, for example, are more closely related to catfish! Baby eels, when they hatch, are usually thin and almost transparent, like glass. They resemble floating silver ribbons. Most have large, bulging eyes and fanglike teeth.

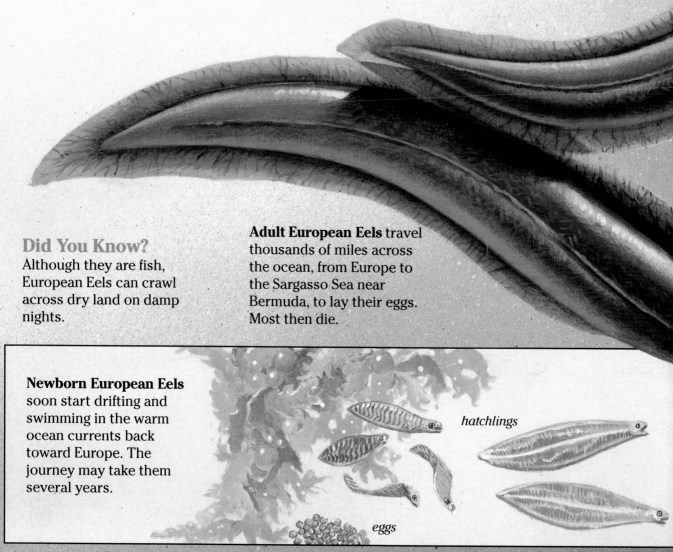

Did You Know?
Although they are fish, European Eels can crawl across dry land on damp nights.

Adult European Eels travel thousands of miles across the ocean, from Europe to the Sargasso Sea near Bermuda, to lay their eggs. Most then die.

Newborn European Eels soon start drifting and swimming in the warm ocean currents back toward Europe. The journey may take them several years.

hatchlings

eggs

Sargasso Sea

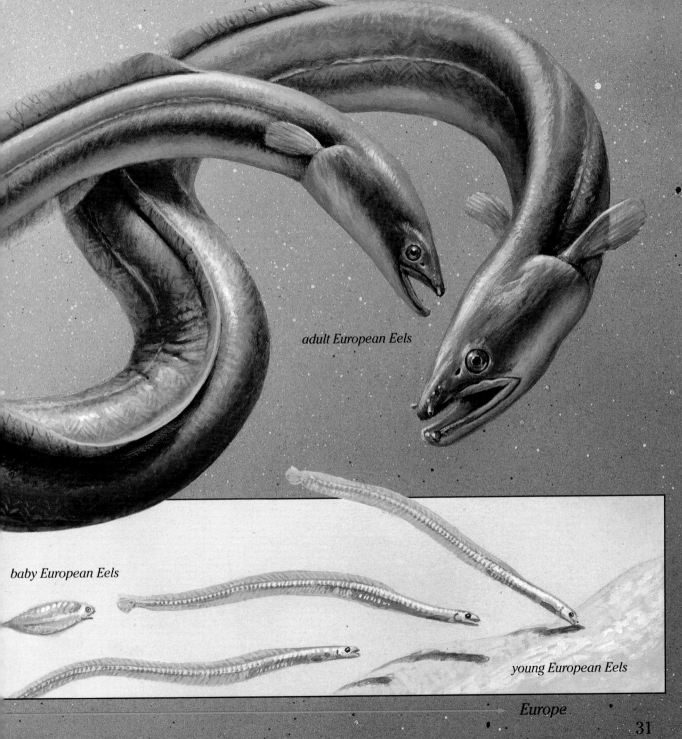

adult European Eels

baby European Eels

young European Eels

Europe

31

Moray Eels

are very common in warm, shallow ocean waters. There are many different kinds and colors of morays. Some have patterns such as spots or stripes and even look a little like sea serpents or other weird sea monsters. In their coral reef homes, morays hide in cracks and holes, waiting to ambush prey. Most have strong jaws and sharp teeth and will usually strike out at their prey, like snakes. Their bite, however, is not poisonous.

Morays have no pectoral fins, and some kinds are more than 6 feet long. The ones shown here are all found near the Bahama Islands in the Caribbean.

Green Moray

Purplemouth Moray

Did You Know?
Morays rely more on smell than sight to locate prey. Beachgoers hoping to feed or just touch those that live in shallow waters might get a nasty bite if their hands smell of fish.

Spotted Moray

Did You Also Know?
If you should ever catch a moray eel, throw it back! The flesh of some morays is poisonous to eat.

33

Garden Eels

Garden Eels live in colonies, inside burrows they dig in the sandy ocean bottom. When it pokes its head out of the burrow, a Garden Eel looks a lot like a blade of sea grass, and the entire colony looks like a garden. Garden Eels almost never leave their burrows completely. They even lay their eggs there and feed on tiny animals slowly drifting past them in the water.

Garden Eels are a favorite food of the Manta Ray. The Manta passes over a colony like a lawnmower, causing the eels to quickly vanish—either by ducking into their burrows to escape or being grabbed up and eaten by the ray!

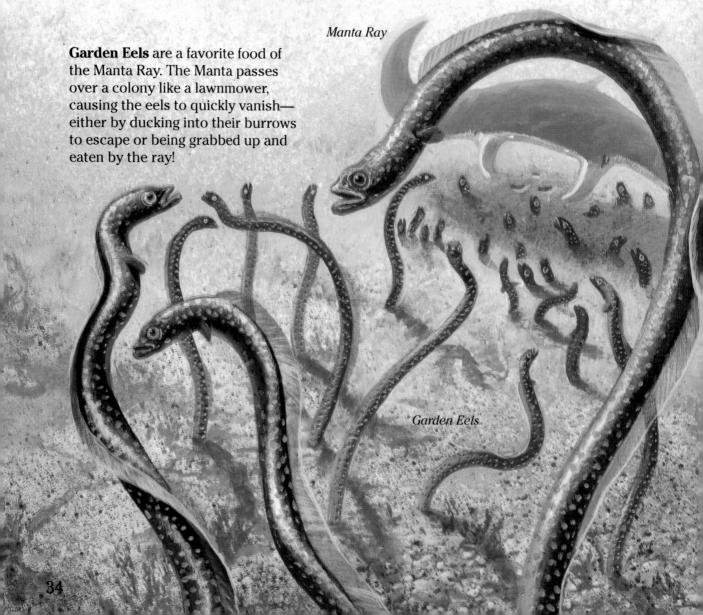

Manta Ray

Garden Eels

Parasitic Snubnosed Eels live in deep ocean waters, where they scavenge for food. If they find a fish resting on the ocean bottom, they may chew a hole in its body, wriggle inside, and temporarily live there! They feed on the fish's flesh and blood. Parasitic Snubnosed Eels have been found inside the flesh of large flatfish and even in the heart of a mako shark!

Parasitic Snubnosed Eels can be more than 2 feet long. That's a lot of eel to carry around! The one seen here is chewing its way into an Angel Shark's flesh.

Angel Shark

Parasitic Snubnosed Eel

For Further Reading

With this book, you've only just begun to explore some exciting new worlds. Why not continue to learn about the fascinating creatures known as sharks, rays, and eels? For example, you might want to browse through *Fishes (A Golden Guide)*, which contains many interesting details on the fish covered in this book and other kinds of fish as well. Another Golden Book you might enjoy is *The Golden Book of Sharks and Whales*. Also, be sure to visit your local library, where you will discover a variety of other titles on the subject.